TEN ACTIVITIES FOR YOUR WELL-BEING

LUIS JORGE

Introduction

The main purpose of this book is to provide activities that will enhance your physical, emotional, mental, and psychological health. It will help you change the stressed and "survival-mode" state of the mind, to the more harmonious and relaxed state of the mind. Therefore, your well-being will improve.

I chose instinctive activities as easy as laughing as well other activities that will bring you harmony and motivation. You can also choose fun and happy activities as well as those that exercise your body. Other options are those that challenge you mentally and intellectually or those that simply relax you.

There are countless activities to enhance your well-being both physically and internally. In this book you will find activities that will improve your brain, your body, and your emotional state of mind. There are also activities that will decrease stress levels therefore enhancing your well-being.

The information found in this book is based on neuroscience, psychology and philosophy.

"Design your own journey; mark your own trail, good luck."

-Luis E. Jorge

Contents

1

Laugh

Laughter has a natural healing capacity. It reduces stress and produces an overall sense of well-being. Laughter can move us into a positive frame of mind.

Laughter also triggers healthy physical changes in the body. Humor and laughter strengthens your immune system, boosts your energy, and protects you from the damaging effects of stress.

Laughter triggers the release of endorphins (the body's natural "feel-good" chemicals). Endorphins promote an overall sense of well-being and can even temporarily relieve pain. Laughter improves the function of blood vessels and increases blood flow, which can help protect you against a heart attack and other cardiovascular problems.

Humor shifts perspective, allowing you to see situations in a more realistic, less threatening light. A humorous perspective creates psychological distance, which can help you avoid feeling overwhelmed.

Humor and playful communication strengthens our relationships by triggering positive feelings and fostering emotional connection. When we laugh with one another, a positive bond is created. This bond acts as a strong buffer against stress, disagreements, and disappointment.

TIP: Go to comedy shows as frequently as you can!

2

Listening to Music and Performing

Music has power, and we need to remember to keep everyone plugged in!

Research indicates that music helps improve cognitive function, increase language development and positive social interaction. Listening to music and performing music impacts the brain as a whole, stimulating both halves of the brain. This improves overall cognitive development and intellectual capacity more than any other activity that affects both sides of the brain simultaneously.

Research shows that gray matter (cortex) volume is highest in professional musicians, intermediate in amateur musicians, and lowest in non-musicians.

A special form of MRI was used to measure the amount of white matter (Cortex) found in the brains of people who practice piano on a regular basis. The findings suggest that practicing the piano is an effective way to enhance the structure of white matter.

A number of different studies have shown that just listening to music can activate areas of the brain involved in:

- **ATTENTION**
- **MEMORY**
- **EXPECTATIONS**
- **Emotion**
- **COORDINATION**

Playing a musical instrument involves multiple components of the central (brain and spinal cord) and peripheral (nerves outside the brain and spinal cord) nervous systems.

As a musician plays an instrument, motor systems in the brain control both gross and fine movements needed to produce sound. The sound is processed by auditory circuitry, which in turn can adjust signaling by the motor control centers. In addition, sensory information from the fingers, hands and arms is sent to the brain for processing. If the musician is reading music, visual information is sent to the brain for processing and interpreting commands for the motor centers. And of course, the brain processes emotional responses to the music as well!

3

Dancing

Dancing is a natural medicine for your brain. For example, in the Albert Einstein College of medicine in New York City, (funded by The National Institute on aging, and published in the New England Journal of medicine) mental acuity in aging was measured. They mainly did this to study Alzheimer disease. They wanted to see if any physical or cognitive recreational activities influence mental acuity. They discovered that some activities had significant benefits while other activities had none. Cognitive activities such as reading books, writing for pleasure, doing crossword puzzles, playing cards and playing musical instruments were measured. They also studied physical activities like playing tennis, golf, swimming, bicycling, dancing, walking and doing house work. One of the surprises of the study was that almost none of the physical activities appeared to offer any protection against dementia. They were cardiovascular benefits, but the focus of this study was the mind.

However, there was one important exception:

The only physical activity to offer protection against dementia was frequent dancing.

Playing Golf 0%

Bicycling and Swimming 0%

Reading 35%

Crossword puzzle at least four days a week 47%

Dancing frequently 76%

That was the greatest risk reduction of dementia of any, cognitive or physical activity studied.

The moral of the story is that dancing integrates several brain functions and has actually been scientifically proven to positively affect your brain. It is a natural healer and will definitely improve your well-being.

4

Mindful Breathing

"Every time you breathe in you have an opportunity to visit the deepest part of yourself. Every time you breathe out you have an opportunity to connect to the world around yourself." -Luis E. Jorge

Our mental, emotional and physical health is all about the quality of oxygen flow in the body.

Since the brain needs about 80% of the oxygen present in the body to function optimally, how you breathe has a huge impact on your mental health and physical well being.

Tension depletes the body's oxygen supply by inhibiting the powerful muscle that supports the lungs, the diaphragm, from sending oxygen to the lower part of the lungs, where it is more effectively released to all parts of the body. At a physical level, deep breathing expands the lungs in ways that allow more oxygen to circulate throughout the body.

Mindful breathing corrects the tendency we have to tense our body, especially around the abdominal muscles.

When depressed or anxious, the breath is shallow, our shoulders are slumped, and lungs are collapsed. We aren't getting enough oxygen rich blood to feed the brain. Deep breathing, along with some adjustments in our posture, allows the lungs to expand to their full capacity so the body and mind receive more oxygen.

Studies show that deep breathing alleviates depression and anxiety, restoring balance to the biochemistry of the brain by raising levels of (*feel-good* hormones) oxytocin, dopamine and prolactin, and lowering levels of cortisol (the stress hor

5

Yoga

Yoga is a science that has been practiced for thousands of years. It consists of ancient theories, observations and principles about the connection of the mind and body. These principles are now being proven by modern medicine. Substantial research has been conducted to look at the health benefits of yoga from the yoga postures (Asanas), yoga breathing (Pranayama), and meditation (Dhyana). The information on yoga poses and benefits are grouped into three categories-physiological, psychological, biochemical effects. Furthermore, scientists have laid these results against the benefits of regular exercise.

A recent Norwegian study found that yoga practice results in changes in gene expression that boost immunity at a cellular level. The researchers believe Yoga also helps to boost immunity by simply increasing overall health, "As you breathe better, move better and circulate better, all the other organs function better." Studies have also found that 12 weeks of yoga can improve sexual desire, arousal, performance, confidence, orgasm and satisfaction for both men and women. Yoga breathing exercises can help you slow down and make better choices when cravings for food strike.

Study by the National Center for Complementary and Alternative Medicine (NCCAM):

One NCCAM-funded study of 90 people with chronic low-back pain found that participants who practiced Iyengar yoga had significantly less disability, pain, and depression after 6 months.

In a 2011 study, also funded by NCCAM, researchers compared yoga with conventional stretching exercises or a self-care book in 228 adults with chronic low-back pain. The results showed that both yoga and stretching were more effective than a self-care book for improving function and reducing symptoms due to chronic low-back pain.

6

Martial Arts

"Martial arts is meditation in motion." -Luis E. Jorge

Martial arts builds self-confidence and a positive attitude that helps to channel aggression. Training martial arts helps you to improve your body physically and psychologically. It also helps your cardio-respiratory function, immune capacity, mental control, flexibility, balance, and coordination.

Martial arts battles stress and anxiety. The Asian martial arts have turned out to be more than tools for self-defense. They have developed into systems that not only protect the practitioner from attackers, but also from poor physical and psychological health.

Since martial art techniques reduce hip impact forces and can be learned by older people, martial arts fall training may prevent hip fractures among people with osteoporosis.

British Journal of Sports Medicine:

Martial arts can reverse and therefore slow the process of aging significantly. The British study showed that the difference in flexibility between the practitioners and the non-practitioners was 114 percent.

Balance becomes extremely important as you age. Thousands of elderly people are injured in falls every year, and as you age the injuries that can result from falls become worse and even life threatening. It is not uncommon to hear of an elderly person who has fallen and broken their hip.

Martial arts is known for it's ability to improve balance, and in some countries it is actively encouraged for older people. Tai Chi is very popular for this purpose. With regard to the British Journal of Sport Medicine study, the balance of the martial artists was more than twice as good as the sedentary group.

7

Massage

The beautiful thing about massage is that you can get all the benefits of yoga, exercise, and music without having to do it yourself. The healing benefits of massage therapy are innumerable; treating chronic pain, stiffness, poor circulation, stress, depression, and more!

Massage is a holistic activity and should not be regarded as mere physical body work. It is always a two-way process and achievement depending on the caring and compassionate way in which it is given.

Massage is a vital necessity for well-being because it promotes homeostasis.

The four divine states of massage:

- Desire to make others happy and the ability to show loving kindness.
- Compassion for all who suffer and a desire to ease their sufferings.

- Rejoice with those who have good fortune and never feel envy.
- Treat everybody equally without prejudice or preference.

Massage also works to ease those sore muscles after a tough workout. Just ten minutes can reduce inflammation, which can help your body recover.

Massage can bring you to a deep state of relaxation, it can also soothe anxiety and depression. Massage reduces levels of stress the hormone (cortisol), resulting in lifted spirits and often lower blood pressure. It can boost the neurotransmitters (serotonin) and (dopamine), which are involved in depression.

Massage also promotes healthy sleep. A number of studies have examined this link. The kind of brain waves released during massage were connected to those of deep sleep.

8

Positive Thinking

What you think about yourself (your self-image) has a great impact on your physical health and on your mental health.

It has been shown that our thoughts and emotions directly affect the state of our physical and mental health. This is called the "mind-body" connection. This connection is made possible because of special chemical messengers, called neuropeptides (small protein-like molecules), which help our body's organs communicate directly with the brain, and vice versa.

Whenever you have a thought or emotion, your brain releases neurotransmitters and hormones, which trigger physical responses in your body. If you are caught in a stressful situation and you react to it with a negative thought, your heart starts racing and your body releases two powerful (stress hormones) cortisol, and adrenalin. When these hormones are secreted in response to continual stress, they have very negative impacts on your body. They accelerate brain aging, increase fat storage, suppress your immune system, and cause muscle and bone loss.

You can't stop external stressors in your life, but you can control your response to them. If you get into the habit of thinking positive thoughts and speaking positive words in negative circumstances (even if the negative thoughts arise), your production of stress hormones will decrease and you will begin to lose body fat more quickly. Positive affirmations will have a great impact on your health and in all aspects of your life.

Develop positive thoughts and attitude. Be polite, speak positive, act positive and live positive!

9

Learning a New Language

Learning a new language causes a great matter of growth in the left inferior frontal gyrus, an area that is active during language processing. Recent investigation shows that learning a new language is a complete mental exercise that requires the participation of all parts of the brain, the medial, anterior, lateral, and posterior orbital. Physiological studies have found that learning a new language is a great asset to the cognitive process. It will help you become smarter by improving the capacity to storage information, memorization, attention and perception. It builds multitasking skills, because they can easily switch between different systems of speech, writing, and structure. It is also a good defense against **Alzheimer's and dementia.**

Several studies have been conducted on this topic, and the results are consistent. For monolingual adults, the mean age for the first signs of dementia is 71.4. For adults who speak two or more languages, the mean age for those first signs is 75.5. Studies considered factors such as education level, income level, gender, and physical health, but the results were consistent.

Learning a new language also helps you become more perceptive. A study from Spain's University of Pompeu Fabra, revealed that multilingual people are better at observing their surroundings. They are more adept at focusing on relevant information and editing out the irrelevant. They're also better at spotting misleading information. According to a study from the University of Chicago, your decision-making skills also improve. This study states that bilinguals tend to make more rational decisions. Any language contains nuance and subtle implications in its vocabulary and these biases can subconsciously influence your judgment. Bilinguals are more confident with their choices after thinking it over in the second language and seeing whether their initial conclusions still stand up.

10

Memory and Brain Exercise

Memory is one of the first survival tools given to humans and animals. There are two important memories encoding in the brain:

- Short-Term memory
- Long-Term memory

The long-term memory is more stable while the short-term memory is more fragile and susceptible to damage. When a movement is repeated over time, a long-term memory is created that eventually will allow to perform a task without conscious effort. This is called muscle memory or (the power of repetition).

Emotion and memories are also connected, the deeper the emotion the more you will remember. People have a tendency to suppress their emotions in order to help them remember more. When someone suppresses their emotions, they isolate a situation which helps the brain remember that specific situation specifically.

For survival purposes, memory has two important tools:

- Thinking
- Emotions

Whenever you are using your memory, you are either thinking or attaching yourself to an emotion. People who don't think will be too emotional and people who are not emotional will be completely thinking, because these are the tools our memory uses instinctively as a way of survival.

The ability a person has to pay attention will improve the capacity of your memory. Brain games, puzzles, and brain teasers, help create new association between different parts of the brain, which keeps it sharp. Challenge yourself to activities with your non-dominant hand like eating or combing your hair to stimulate your weakest part of your brain.

The story of Anatoly Sharansky is a great story. He was a soviet human rights activist, who was locked away in a Russian prison for nine years, spending a lot of time alone in a darkened tiny cell. While he was in jail he thought to challenge his brain so he decided to mentally play chess. Sharansky obsessively played mental chess using both sides of the game, and this activity probably kept him sane and helped him to survive. Of course this intense focus on chess made him become an expert. He even won against Garry Kasparov at a later game. In this story we see how mental practice is one of the most advanced forms of brain exercises.

Here are some recommendations for your well-being.

- Stay intellectually active
- Keep yourself physically active
- Socialize more
- Relax more
- Sleep at least 7 to 8 hours
- Avoid stress
- Eat healthy

Glossary

Endorphins: *They are produced by the central nervous system and pituitary gland. Endorphins are among the brain chemicals known as neurotransmitters, which function to transmit electrical signals within the nervous system.*

Well-being*:* *the state of being comfortable, healthy, happy, and positive. It is an internal and external harmonious balance between mind, body and soul.*

Cognitive: *Cognition is by humans conscious and unconscious, concrete or abstract, as well as intuitive and conceptual. Cognitive processes use existing knowledge and generate new knowledge.*

Gray matter cortex: *(lat.* ***Substantia grisea****) is a major component of the central nervous system, consisting of neuronal cell bodies, neuropil (dendrites and myelinated as well as* *unmyelinated axons), glial cells (astroglia and oligodendrocytes) and capillaries. It is primarily associated with processing and cognition.*

White matter cortex: *consists mostly of glial cells and myelinated axons that transmit signals from one region of the cerebrum to another and between the cerebrum and lower brain centers. White matter modulates the distribution of action potentials, acting as a relay and coordinating communication between different brain regions.*

Mental acuity: *Mental acuity is sharpness of the mind which involved memory, focus, concentration, and understanding.*

Homeostasis: *It is a process that maintains the stability of the human body's internal environment in response to changes in external conditions.*

Delta waves: *It is a high amplitude brain wave with a frequency of oscillation between 0–4 hertz. Delta waves, like other brain waves, are recorded with an electroencephalogram[1] (EEG) and are usually associated with the deep stage 3 of NREM sleep, also known as slow-wave sleep (SWS), and aid in characterizing the depth of sleep.*

Neuropeptides: They are small protein-like molecules (peptides) used by neurons to communicate with each other. They are neuronal signaling molecules that influence the activity of the brain in specific ways. Different neuropeptides are involved in a wide range of brain functions, including analgesia, reward, food intake, metabolism, reproduction, social behaviors, learning and memory.

Gyrus: *(pl. gyri) It is a ridge on the cerebral cortex. It is generally surrounded by one or more sulci (depressions or furrows; sg. sulcus).*

Suppress: *Prevent the development, action, or expression of (a feeling, impulse, idea, etc.); restrain.*

SOURCES

- Barnes PM, Bloom B, Nahin RL. Complementary and alternative medicine use among adults and children: United States, 2007. *CDC National Health Statistics Report #12.* 2008.

- Williams K, Abildso C, Steinberg L, et al. Evaluation of the effectiveness and efficacy of Iyengar yoga therapy on chronic low back pain. *Spine.* 2009;34(19):2066–2076.

- Legg, R. (2009). Using music to accelerate language learning: an experimental study. Research in Education, (82), 1-12. Retrieved from the Professional Development Collection database.

- Williams, Linda. Teaching for the two-sided mind: a guide to right brain/left brain education. Simon & Schuster. 1986.

- Schellenberg, E. (2005). Music and Cognitive Abilities. Current Directions in Psychological Science (Wiley-Blackwell). 317-320
- Burriss, Kathleen Glascott; Strickland, Susan J. (2001). "Review of Research: Music and the Brain in Childhood Development". *Childhood Education* 78 (2): 100.
- DrDouris New York Institute of Technology, PO Box 8000, Northern Boulevard, Old Westbury, NY 11568, USA; pdouris@nyit.edu
- Doidge, N. 2007. *The Brain That Changes Itself:* Stories of Personal Triumph from theFrontiers of Brain Science. *New York:Viking.*
- Anne Merritt, (19 Jun 2013). The Telegraph, benefits of bilingualism Saturday 30, august 2014.

www.ingramcontent.com/pod-product-compliance
Lightning Source LLC
Chambersburg PA
CBHW070843310526
45793CB00011B/524
9781505532982